Haiku and Other Short Poetic Thoughts

EG Ted Davis

ISBN: 978-93-6354-782-7

First Edition: 2025
Rs. 200/-

Cyberwit.net
HIG 45 Kaushambi Kunj, Kalindipuram
Allahabad - 211011 (U.P.) India
http://www.cyberwit.net
Tel: +(91) 9415091004
E-mail: info@cyberwit.net

Printed at Repro India Limited.

Traverse your own mind
discover the stars within
allow the Light in

To accept or reject

Here,
before your eyes,
the writ is presented,
the time for decision
has finally arrived...

Do you accept it...

or do you *reject* it.

Lend

A divided nation,
A divided people,

shall lend itself
to its enemies.

That Bridge

I crossed that bridge today,
the one where arrogance and
ignorance collided head on...
and devastated two children's lives.

2.

Kill not innocence
with your bombs of destruction
with false intentions

They say

Some say it's just a story,
others say it's a feeling,
while a minute few of us...

are in the know.

Focus

All those stupid people.

Then I have to reflect
into my own mental mirror,

and ask myself,

am I really all that
much smarter than they.

The root

Disease can be attributed
to man's feeble attempts
at manipulating nature.

Eternal purpose

For service
unto thyself...
serves no
eternal purpose.

3.

Amazon driver
scanning and photographing
modern day hero

Tears

Tears...

an outward expression
of our internal Being.

I

I sought You
and I found greatness.
A greatness missed
by those who seek You not.

Reconciliation

One may not be
able to change
the events of the past...

but one can reconcile.

I attempt to eat

I eat my bowl of cornflakes
(or should I say, I attempt)-
with feline' assistance
(with feline' persistence).

Meaningless words spoke
out of anger and vengeance
forgiveness needed

4.

Those private matters
those of the old Mad Hatter
what do they matter

In Crisis

In times of crisis,
dig deep within your spirit,
and comforting words
shall swell up from within.

Damn Folly

Let me partake
not in folly,
for folly is
entry into
damnation.

The sad truth

It saddens me,
it saddens you,
when we tell stories
filled with saddened truths.

To die for thought

The mind
will push the body...

to the brink of
a cardiac arrest.

He consumes little
self inflicted starvation
A dead man walking

5.

Prophesy to us
tell us who has struck Your face
Grimace He did not

We

...of the
industrialized nations
are glutinous
without thanksgiving.

Who is next

Hong Kong,
where has your freedom gone,
the CCP...
they've taken it away.

Canceled

Youth of Yesteryear
        -Arise-
Drape yourselves in
Patriotic Colors...

Before the future
generations cancel
you forever.

A riddled fiddle

Play me a riddle
across the strings
of the old fiddle.

Let the bow pull and
push across the strings,
play me the riddle
and what it shall bring.

6.

I call out to You
again, again and again
thrice You answer not

Devoured

Once the flesh
has tasted of pleasure,
it will attempt to
devour the
spirit's resistance.

Done

One cannot change
the deeds done-
the words spoken-
from their past,

but one can indeed...

reconcile.

To Commune

The clutter within the mind-
stifles the opportunities
to commune with the Creator.

Our Creator

Nothing shall ever
be any greater...

than its creator

Through Creation's eyes
we are ants on an anthill
give us some sugar

7.

Bountiful harvest
not that of grains grapes or figs
but that of lost souls

Good and Evil

The poetics reside
within the mind...
awaiting to be released
by good or...

by evil.

Truth and Lies

That which lies behind us
is a lie...
that which lies ahead of us...

is, indeed, the truth.

Dig Deep

One must dig deeper...
or otherwise they shall find

their spiritual trousers down
around their fleshly ankles.

Adhesion

Let us be
divided no more...

Let us come together...

Let us stick together...
adhesion, adhesion...adhesion

8.

meat over nectar
not all bees land in heaven
some are toilet flushed

Wasted

Oh such fortune,
oh such luxury,
all laid to waste in
a moment of time.

In Service

We, who bear arms,
who dawn a
battle uniform...

serve at the pleasure...

of both the believer
and the unbeliever.

The loss of angels

The busy-ness of life
separates our spiritual eyes
from the angelic beings.

The truth about destroying a virus

To eradicate,
to exterminate,
one must...

Burn It.

9.

Texas Ebony tree
thorny spikes guard your branches
wildlife dare not feast

The Truth

Escaping containment of
experiments purposely manipulated...
gone astray
through careless...

handling.

Time

Is our Time
the End of Time,
or the beginning...leading
up to the End of Time.

To now cower

Shall I cower
away from the Word
that preserves life...

most certainly not.

Awareness

I need to be less
aware of that
which is visibly
around me...

and more aware
of that that is
around me invisibly.

10.

Inauguration
changing of the policies
nation divided.

Inspired

There is inspiration,
and then there is...

Divine Inspiration.

Behavior

If it were the correct behavior,
wouldn't the majority be...

behaving in the same manner.

Actions

And to think if the
actions taken were
the correct actions
to be taken...

one would think...
the majority would follow...

and perform the same.

The ashes

I should not feel
the presence of
those who've been
burned to ashes...

but feel only
the comforting presence
of the One...

who created them.

11.

The cycle begins
blue vs red and vice versa
cast ye your ballot

Forward looking

When you are shown things
that create that much hope...
how can one look at
that which is behind them.

From dust to dust

As we allow dust
to collect upon our
shelves and upon
our wares,

so, too,

do we allow dust
to collect upon
ourselves and
upon our lives.

These rags I wear

Cast me not from Your sight-
banish me not from Your power-
even though my soul be clothed
by these fleshly-and sinful-rags.

Crimson clover blooms
bee activity begins
such a sweet honey

Come now small dogs
frolic in the snow of spring
soon the sun shall blaze

12.

I have chosen her
I should have chosen another
for she provokes me

Consider this also

Had there been no greed,
had there been no importation,
think how much different...

America's history would be.

Grounded

One shall do wrong-
when one's mind is
not grounded in...

righteousness.

Influential

The brain;
when influenced by the spirit,
becomes a very powerful tool.

Created downfall

What we consume
by what our
hands have manipulated...

shall certainly be
our downfall.

Chapel bells tolling
morning Robins still themselves
thunder rolls overhead

13.

Implosion coming
economic loss is looming
Where is Old Glory

Where credit is due

And if You
give me such...
shall I be ignorant
and not give You
the justifiable credit.

Crafty Writings

And one wonders
    why a word crafter worries-
        for even judgment comes upon them
    for their carelessly
written crafts.

The evil within the mind

It is within the mind;
where the illusions begin,
where temptation sets in,

where fantasy lays dormant...

and where evil roams.

An old Scribe

Age and experience
makes us better scribes
of history's past.

Hair is in turmoil
aging factor has set in
still youthful at heart

14.

Crab Apples drop down
someone shall scavenge this fruit
jelly there shall be

Strong faith

Do we have that
kind of faith,
or does it get
clouded up by Doubt.

When

When does discrimination slow,
when does gun violence slow,

only when the government
regulates the software manufacturers...

and the movie producers.

The cause of Cancer

Cancers are the results
of man's manipulation
of all things naturally raw...

and digging up what
man was never intended
to be digging up.

---

in the beginning
there was great hope-true love
Technology steals

We take no new breaths
we communicate no more
the black hearse arrives

15.

Through Creation's eyes
we are ants on an anthill
give us some sugar

Today's Choice

If I had but one
choice this day
I would choose...

redemption.

2 Words

Fragmented mind,
shattered dreams,
petals fall,
seeds germinate,
inflated ego,
deflated footballs,
hope lost,
redemption found.

A glimpse

As temptation from
within the loins has
dissolved with age,
it is then that
I fully realize what
eternity shall be like.

A Headache means

Headache...

Payback for
negative thinking.

16.

Good verses Evil
which shall overpower which
Choose whom to follow

Thoughts

I find myself angered-
horrified by violent thoughts,
as I cross over the bridge
of secular thinking.

Within the poet's pen

And within the realms
of free verse, prose and poetry,
we commit the writer's greatest crime-
we are allowed to intermingle
fact with fiction.

I need to go now (like right now)

Perceived dreamed fears are
introduced when the need to urinate-
is greater than
the privilege of sleep.

No graying vanity

I color not my hair
(for vanity shall not enter in)

or so says

my wife

17.

This is not by chance
this is by unique design
Human existence

The Spin Room

They call it the Spin Room.

A place where journalists
attempt to swap wits,
and do nothing
more than irritate
their audience.

Feline insight

Could this be the actual heart attack,
could the feline be sensing its coming-
as she kneads my chest area.

The stench of humankind

There'd be no
nauseous odors,
if there were
no humankind.

Wisdom

It is wisdom
to practice
what we write.

Justice shall prevail
The sentence shall be quite harsh
Eternal torment

18.

Water now frozen
a glass pane upon the lake
ice fishing begins

Our thoughts

Let our thoughts always
be spiritually wholesome.

The Art of Verse

To say for others...
that which they cannot
say for themselves.

To be forever yoked

In the present,
my male animal self
sizes her up physically,

when I should be sizing
up her eternal spirit.

The flock

Lead your flock down
the path of righteousness,
allow not your flock
to lead you astray.

The deception

Allow me not to sin,
as secular music
comes into my earbuds,

as memories of
older sins attempt
to slip their way in.

19.

Apple tree in blossom
and soon ripe fruit shall appear
the pin rolls the dough

Right writing

I write,
I write not,
but I must write...

about that
which is Right.

Governmental threat

What is a threat
towards national security...

it is when
the government
feels threatened
by it's own citizens.

Matters

Curse the sun,
embrace the moon,
heat over chill;
is quickly one's doom.

I am

My patience grows thin-
with the materialism
which surrounds me
in gross amounts,

for I am a...

Hoarder

20.

Alfalfa in bales
sagebrush is now in full bloom
winter is coming

Asking

Ask the Almighty to
look after the two of you;

for one is meek and mild...
while the other is erratic and wild.

Are they

Are they indeed
holier than we are,
or has their holier than thou
attitude truly blinded them.

To seek

Is it wisdom I seek,
or should I rather be seeking...

spiritual insight.

Deep decisions

If your mind perceives it,
do you really want to do it...

or even say it.

Let us not

We shall do just
fine with technology,
as long as it does not...

lead us into temptation

20.

Politically
blinded by false rhetoric
ballots await us

Realities

And someday
I shall
pass away
from this reality
to the next
Real...ality.

Within the nighttime darkness

At night;
my spirit steps out
-while my physical sleeps-
and walks upon
hollowed ground.

Traveling

One must enjoy the
landscape's ugliness
to truly enjoy its beauty.

Challenging times

In times of the
greatest challenges,
He is with us.

Time passes

For as we age,
so shall this planet,
for all has a time of beginning,
and all has a time of ending.

21.

Return to the ground
that which has come from the ground
Sakura blossom

And this generation

For it is the greatest story told-
over and over again,
good over evil,
told over and over-
without wavering...
interpreted via repetition

by generations of minds.

Created

No, we're not!

See... right there-
my point exactly,

You've been deceived.

To Be

We are here to reproduce
in order to be introduced

(to accept or
to reject)

to the God
who created us.

Recession com-meth
Food fuel now priorities
Shopping sprees end-eth

22.

Drive away darkness
surround us with Your brightness
bestow your blessings

My angel

My angel is
one step in
front of me
in all that
I do, say,
or think.

To cherish Thee

How shall I know
that You cherish me
as a child of Yours,
if I fail to
commune with Thee.

The hard truth

I'm not here to
soften the truth...

either you decide
you're in...or...

you're out.

To act

Whether in or
out of fellowship,
act as a disciplined follower...

not as an undisciplined child.

23.

Anything that is less
bears Our souls as unworthy
We must be All in

Confession

For I have sinned,
I confess,
and a voice answers back...

See, now you're catching on.

To be properly led

Let not man lead us into
the bowels of banishment.
Let only our creator
lead us into the
bliss of forever.

The next step

We must speak of the afterlife,
for if we do not...

how shall we know how to face it.

Proverb of Giving

Let yourself be a cheerful giver...
but be wise in your giving.

Toying

Let not my
mind toy with folly
and the damnation it brings.

24.

Radio is off
Television also off
Communion is on.

To matter

Human matters
matter not,
only God's
matters matter

The truth in tradition

One shall find themselves
following taught traditions,

but do those traditions
lead to eternal truths.

To truly see

Thus, let us
be found worthy,

so that we may
be able to see
that which we
now cannot see.

Two Lines

Ministry is about sacrifice,
not about secular comforts.

You are the reason
I am what I have become
Hell shutters in fear

25.

Disinterested
in the professors lecture
my K-9 beckons

Powerful wording

Six of the most
powerful words...

We
are
created...
in
His
Image.

Unto no other

Baptize them unto
The Father,
The Son,
The Holy Spirit,
and unto...

no other.

My soul's bound for

When this lifetime
comes to a conclusion...

I know where
the best part of
me is going.

Small fruits harvested,
huckleberry pie baking...
the blackbirds rejoice.

26

cucumbers mature
the pot boils the solution
pickles for winter

His Power

The power of
the Almighty God...

is...

to be feared
-and-
to be revered.

Forgiveness sought

May You
forgive me
for allowing
the secular
to get in the way
of the spiritual.

Soul's salvation

For only one thing
matters in this life...

The preservation
of souls.

The least we...

could do is
be grateful
and give
thanks for
what He has
provided us.

27.

Trout upon the dock
flip flopping around wildly
short on oxygen

Distant lights

Faraway galaxies
are meaningless,
as they shall pass
away just as the
Earth shall pass away
in forthcoming days.

He lives

Because of
the emptiness
of that tomb,
we can have the
peace of mind,

to know that He
is indeed alive.

Focus upon Him

If I focus not
upon Him,
my mind shall-
and will...

wander.

Righteous

All things are possible-
through Him-
if they are of a...

righteous nature.

28.

I ponder dying
as Robins sing out above
Trees sway to their hymns

Setting my mind

And when the Tempter
calls me out,
I do just as Jesus
would have done...

and set my mind
upon the Father.

Authoritative words

Words taught with authority,
not an authority from His mother's womb,
but with authority from His Father's spirit.

Writing poetry

The Quill shall not be
dipped into the Ink Well
until the Spirit...

has Spoken.

Dying

For it is the
hearing of Death's
tolling bells...

that plagues the mind and
destroys the human will.

Peach tree in blossom
awaiting pollination
honey bees hover

29.

We before the Judge
our Attorney is present
there is no jury

Power

The most powerful
position in the world-
is meaningless if the
planet becomes uninhabitable.

And she

How dare I cheat my tithe,
for I have been blessed
with great prosperity,

while she gave all she had,
potentially leading to starvation.

Priority of prayer

For the deceased-
I cannot pray for.

But for the living
I shall pray for...

fervently.

Blackened Gold

Golden is Thee who
endures and waits patiently,
Blackened is Thee
who scoffs and doubts.

Persecution comes
before the promise returns
for it is written

30.

Shall we be awake
when the horse drawn hearse arrives
nightmares as we sleep

Consequences

When complacency
expands within a free society,

then dictatorship shall
certainly follow.

Man's own Loss

Today-the phone is slid
into the back pocket,
as the sacred billfold
was in days gone by-
yet...

the loss is
just the same.

We are

We are unified-
and without division-
if we only believe...

in one nation
under one God.

Graciousness

Oh Heavenly Father...

I give thanks
as I sit-

soaking in the beauty...

of Your creation.

31.

Wheat is harvested
Weeds are cast into the fire
which choice do we make

That Day of Resurrection

For today-
he wrote a check
to pay for the place
his bones shall rest,
awaiting that glorious day-
that day of Returning...

that Day of Resurrection.

Walking on sand

The path least traveled
upon the ocean's bottom-
as waters parted
and Israel passed
    -while-
their enemies drowned

Substance

Why worry of
what I shall consume-
for at a minimum
dairy and grains
shall sustain,
though flavorings
delight the
taste buds.

---

to stifle a gift
is spiritually sinful
angels in dismay

32.

The Constitution
should be Our Constitution
declare ownership

Indeed thankful

It is indeed by
Your shed blood
that I am saved...

and for that I
am indeed thankful.

One of Them

And when He returns He'll
say *I knew you not.*

Be sure you are
not one of them.

To Commune

The clutter within the mind-
stifles the opportunities
to commune with the Creator.

Japanese forward thinking

And once again
imports shall soar,
by consumer demand,
as hydrogen gains
power in Japan.

Candle Factory
what once made windows glow
now lays in darkness

33.

Minds bound by their sins
derangement derails their thoughts
reset the filters

A day is like

For a thousand years,
ten generations have
faithfully served the Lord-

and He nodded in approval,
for only a Day had passed.

Look

Cling not
to false hope
of this life...

but look forward
to true hope
in the hereafter.

Hiding

I may hide
from my spouse
behind the
Maple tree...

but from God...

that tactic
never works.

Mercy shown to me
thanksgiving I shall sing
for such receiving

34.

I bow down my head
and give thanksgiving to He
who is the Greater

No matter...

No matter what you're doing,
No matter where you're at,
it all shall come...

to a Conclusion.

The Aunt

I haunt,
you taunt,

together,
we flaunt.

My prayers

I would pray for
you this day, my friend,
except you are deceased.

And now my prayers
are no longer effective,
and no longer within your reach.

A brief note to Jesus (during the election season)

I shall Elect You
to carry my burdens...
and my pains.

The word happiness
shall it follow deep sorrow
or preempt sadness

35.

The First are promised
They walk in the ways of Old
the Rest are redeemed

Time elapses

I lavish not the sounds
of the wind up clock,
each tick, each tock...

taking life's time away-
each and every day.

To confess

At the moment you sin,
choose not to hold it within,
but right then and there...

confess it for
Him to hear.

Envision

How can one envision God,
if one does not believe in Him.

Our lives

Our lives are not our own-
we can either choose
to rebel against that
or we can embrace it.

No more Magicians
or Sorcerers in my dreams
visualizing Him

One shall not condemn
the person nor condone their
willing sinfulness.

36.

Young large built bully
walking with an attitude
Hell awaits his soul

True unification

If the heads of all nations
should raise their hands in worship...
would this not
be *true unification.*

Come participate

Fruit of the vine
within the cup,
bread awaits
upon the table...

Come-participate.

Soul assassination

If they choose not to
depart from their evil ways,
it shall not be we who
assassinate their souls,

but it shall be He
who has the power
to assassinate all of our souls.

Deceived by Deception

I ask myself-
why have I so many
thoughts of deception,
and then I realize
that the majority
of those who
surround me
are grossly...

deceived.

37.

Food is nothing more
than to fuel the covering
of your very soul.

Nothing has changed

I looked up at the Cross this day...

A weapon used in an attempt
to kill Your Son's flesh
by the terrorists of His era...

and I look through the news
headlines today and realize...

that nothing has changed.

You talk

You talk
a good talk...
but have you added...
unto the flock.

Dip into

Dip into the
spiritual well
and spiritual
answers shall
spring forth.

For

For You brought
the visible forth
from the invisible...

how awesome
is Your power.

38.

Let my mind quiet
allow my spirit to soar
there I shall find peace

I am...

...forever grateful
to Him who gives us

the promise of...

eternal life.

The burning of the weeds

I would rather be wheat
and be harvested,
than to be bundled as
a weed and be burned.

Concerns

Take the weight of
these secular concerns
off of my mind...

for the concerns of God
outweigh the concerns of man.

From within my roots

For the roots
of my genealogy
call me out-
to share the word of
our Lord Jesus Christ.

Where the bombs landed
devastation is present
how long before peace

39.

They believe a lie
and perish into darkness
Evilness prevails

My place within

He's shown me the
corrective action I must take...
to receive a place
within His Kingdom.

Faith

I confess my faith
with the ink pen

...upon this ruled
sheet of paper.

Banishment

Let not the
temptation of this
world devour me,
lest I be

banished forever
from Your sight.

Centered

Let us not lean
so far left,

or so far right,

that we fail to
stay centered...

upon scripture.

40.

We all partake in
meals and digesting our food
along with our words

The orphan

For even if one is barren,
if one is childless,
life can be still fulfilled
if one raises up...

the orphan.

Redemption by name

Call me out,
by name,
for if You do,
then I know
without a doubt,
I am indeed...

redeemed.

Your eternity

Let us give thanksgiving to Thee,
Let us praise Thee,
Let us rejoice in Thee,
Let us trust in Thee...

on our way...

into Your...eternity.

That holy veil that
hides the invisible realm
let us peer behind

41.

We can rightfully
shame them by voting them out
then change shall take place.

Come

So much power
available to us,
yet, foolishly-
we seek it not...

O' come
O' Holy Spirit

The two

He spoke to
His only Son
before all that
is visible was...

Let us make man
after our own Image.

Anger Management

Anger is an instinct found
inherent in all humans,
just make sure yours is...

Righteous Anger.

Overcoming

If you truly follow Jesus,
just as Jesus followed the Father,
then you, also, can become an...

Overcomer.

42.

Irrationals lead
no bipartisanship found
Economy's gone

Thy mate

If the mate
that you love is
laying beside you...

you will always
sleep a
whole lot better.

Purity

Nothing of purity
is produced by the
hands of humans,

only such pureness
can be produced by
the hand of God.

Him

Read me the scripture
which tells of the
immaculate conception,
reminding me of why
I follow Him who was
immaculately conceived.

Severed Connections

Be not concerned
if connectivity to the
internet is severed
-instead-
be greatly concerned
if connectivity to the
spiritual is severed.

www.ingramcontent.com/pod-product-compliance
Lightning Source LLC
LaVergne TN
LVHW091122150826
845673LV00002B/931